CLOTHESLINES

CLOTHESLINES

A COLLECTION OF POETRY & ART

Edited by Stan Tymorek

HARRY N. ABRAMS, INC., PUBLISHERS

INTRODUCTION

The first verses about clothing that I ever heard were sung by a gyrating young man on television who was very attached to his blue suede shoes. Soon afterward, in first grade, a sweet nun read our class a poem I remember as "New shoes, new shoes/Red and white and blue shoes/Tell me which would you choose/If you were to buy." Those two takes on shoes, which Charles Simic praises on page 52 for their "mute patience," foreshadowed the diverse approaches to clothing found in this collection.

Growing up in a family with two older sisters and a mother who not only paid close attention to clothing styles, but also sewed many of their own outfits, surely heightened my awareness of apparel. I remember my sister Judy clueing me in on how to make my parochial school uniform look "cool" – no mean feat given the required white shirt and mud brown pants and tie – by wearing penny loafers and white socks. Of course, the effect was not as cool as the look attained by the Parisian *zazou* with white socks on page 89, but then I never tried striking his finger-pointing pose. Fortunately for my sisters and me, my mother could affordably indulge our eye for style with her employee discount at our suburban New Jersey branch of Bloomingdale's, where she tracked the marking down of prices with the diligence of a stockbroker waiting to buy low.

Years later, I was happy to carry on the family tradition by providing my own children with a well-used discount on clothing while I worked as a copywriter for the Lands' End catalog. In that era *fashion* was the F-word and *utility* was enshrined as the corporate muse. But I needed more than her inspiration when, as a fledgling copywriter, I had to sell a men's plaid sportcoat that could best be described as, in contrast to Simic's shoes, loud. One art director, seeing me at a loss for words, unhelpfully called it a "horse blanket." To this day I would defy any one of the poets in this collection to make that sportjacket's copy "sing."

Given my background, it isn't surprising that the insights into clothing that I came across while reading made a lasting impression. In "The Dawn In Erewhon," a story with characters who spend most of their time joyously naked, Guy Davenport quotes a Russian formalist: "Life flows, Viktor Shklovksy says, in staccato pieces belonging to different systems. And adds: only our clothing, not the body, joins together the disparate moments of life. Clothes are symbols and constitute a system, a language. Clothes say that we reserve to ourselves the symbol of our body as fate." In another story Davenport points out that the

Japanese even have a word for one of his character's favorite leather jacket: "*wabi*," an accustomed and familiar garment, as comfortable as a sock."

But what of the charge so often leveled against clothing, and fashion in particular: that it is all vanity? The contributors Calvin Trillin, John Updike, and two anonymous Regency poets poke fun at the excesses of "the rag trade." And yet it's hard to deny the beauty of a Chanel dress, as celebrated by Pamela White Hada's poem (page 46); or the elaborate Japanese geisha costumes that still manage to mirror nature (pages 68–69); or the truth of this fashion statement by Remy Saisselin in her article "Baudelaire to Christian Dior: The Poetics of Fashion": "... let us admit that a dress may be at some moment of its existence, a poem of form, color and motion, and that at such a privileged instant the dress may transform the wearer into a poetic apparition." Taking this metaphor of dress-as-poem quite literally, Sonia Delaunay designed and wore a dress with the text of a poem by the Dadaist Tristan Tzara sewn right into it.

If you need further assurance that clothing is not frivolous before simply enjoying the matched pairs of poems and artwork that follow, consider the work of the classics scholar and great contemporary poet Anne Carson. In a *New York Times Magazine* profile of her last year, Carson described seeing Catherine Deneuve playing a philosophy professor in a movie and wearing a sweater just like one of the poet's. The connection led Carson to write a poem/essay on "My Life As Catherine Deneuve." In another recent poem she "dives into the mind of her deceased father" by slipping on his blue cardigan. "Sweaters are key," Carson said in the *Times.* "You inhabit somebody through their sweater."

Of course a more common way to inhabit other people is through art. And so I invite you to try these poems and images on for size.

— S. T.

GIRL AND FRIENDS VIEW NAKED GODDESS

Molly Peacock

She'd rather be nude, she'd rather be dressed,
rather cover up her bum and breasts.
If she dropped her clothes would she look like *this?*
A sculpted goddess, bare as an almond?
Her girlfriends' buzz about those goddess tits,
though the shy one stares straight ahead – stunned
to see what she might become. What might
the goddess become if she could untighten
her gaze and be part of her watchers' scene?
Ruffled, laced, stockinged and corseted,
this girl's dying to shed it all; a sheen
of longing on her face asks, "Can't I be rid
of my stays?" But the object she'd become
would have to stay in the hall alone

in the clammy gloom of every Roman night...
Goddess, her ideal, may you not feel
or have to possess a soul... Let that light
inside these girls, who'll dash down the hall
with arms linked, out for a bite to eat and
lots of gossip at their visits end
(for now they've seen her, and she's inside them,
a man's ideal, and they see they could be she,
the naked lady of a sculptor's whim.
cold as the floors they walk on), let that light glow.
May they dress up daily, may their servants stir
hot washtubs of bloody cotton strips to insure
they won't bleed on their taffetas. May they laugh
at a man inserting his soul in a sculpture.
May the sculpture not feel it intrude there,
and chafe. And may her observers be creatures.

Pier Celestino Gilardi
A VISIT TO THE GALLERY
1877. Oil on canvas, 40⅝ x 32⅞". University of
Michigan Museum of Art. Bequest of Henry C. Lewis.

"Body is to spirit"
Laurance Wieder

Body is to spirit
As cloth is to body
Grown to its own size:
Room in the air,
Air in the weave.
Waves in the breeze.
The earth spins and
Things come to an end.
So, day and night,
A body blooms
At its own hour.
Stretch the pause
Through the sky.
Or float – muted banner –
Signs, no designs.

Signs, no designs
Or float – muted banner –
Through the sky,
Stretch the pause
At its own hour.
A body blooms
So, day and night,
Things come to an end.
The earth spins and
Waves in the breeze.
Air in the weave.
Room in the air,
Grown to its own size:
As cloth is to body
Body is to spirit.

Cecil Beaton
TWIGGY

*1967. Courtesy of Sotheby's
Picture Library, London*

VALENTINE

Robert Creeley

Had you a dress
would cover you all
in beautiful echoes
of all the flowers I know,

could you come back again,
bones and all,
just to talk
in whatever sound,

like letters spelling words,
this one says, *Mother,*
I love you –
that one, *my son.*

Gustav Klimt
PORTRAIT OF EUGENIA PRIMAVESI

1913–14. Oil on canvas, 55⅛ x 33¼".
Toyota Municipal Museum of Art, Japan

THE NEW DRESS

Linda Zisquit

Unable to sleep
I step into the bath.
A small mirror leans
against the sink, its surface
a pattern of breasts, belly, hair,
bones rising through a wet
silk veil. I'll hold my breath,
watch myself loosen in the soft spray.

I remember children dressing,
someone crying, their need to leave
gathering sweat inside my robe.
I see them drift from me again,
press the nozzle close
as if its motion would fill,
trace light disappearing on my skin,
and leaves on the window
like voices.

It all comes back:
looking out,
pulled by a blade of grass,
the frame where another woman bends
hanging out wash. I'll go
to town, wind my loss into
fabric, a dress of cotton gauze.

Water breaks the image.
I start to whistle in the tub,
stroke my back with a bristle stick.
And still my face
eludes the mirror like a moon,
unreflected disc
waiting for breath above water,
wanting under, wanting to lie
on the bottom of rock and blue marina.

I am only flesh, a surface
caressed in all its folds
as if the new dress were a sign
and the crowds in tomorrow's city
so many ruffles against my skin.
Clean, I am so clean–
my skin translucent,
my body the only achievement.

Dalia Katav-Arieli
DRESS

2000. Pencil on paper, 39⅜ x 27½".
Courtesy of the artist

SEWING A DRESS

Lorine Niedecker

The need
these closed-in days

to move before you
smooth-draped
and color-elated

in a favorable wind

BLACK

Grace Nichols

Show me the woman
that would surrender
her little black dress
to a white-robed clan
and I would show you a liar.

Not for their bonfire,
her wardrobe saviour
the number
in which she comes
into her own power.

Go to a funeral
in black and know
that the dead
beside the white candles
will not be offended.

Add amber earrings,
perhaps a hat or scarf of pink
and know you are ready –
for a wedding.
How black absorbs everything.

Stand around at a party
in black – you are your own artist,
your own sensual catalyst,
surprised to say the least
when black brings you

Those sudden inexplicable hostile glances.

Jan Tymorek
JULIE IN BLACK EVENING GOWN

2000

max ernst

bedecktsamiger stapel-
mensch nacktsamiger wasserformer
(ordelformer) kleidsame nervatur
auch
! umpress nerven!
(c'est le chapeau qui fait l'homme)
(le style c'est le tailleur)

EXCHANGING HATS

Elizabeth Bishop

Unfunny uncles who insist
in trying on a lady's hat,
 — oh, even if the joke falls flat,
we share your slight transvestite twist

in spite of our embarrassment.
Costume and custom are complex.
The headgear of the other sex
inspires us to experiment.

Anandrous aunts, who, at the beach
with paper plates upon your laps,
keep putting on the yachtsmen's caps
with exhibitionistic screech,

the visors hanging o'er the ear
so that the golden anchors drag,
 — the tides of fashion never lag.
Such caps may not be worn next year.

Or you who don the paper plate
itself, and put some grapes upon it,
or sport the Indian's feather bonnet,
 — perversities may aggravate

the natural madness of the hatter.
And if the opera hats collapse
and crowns grow draughty, then, perhaps,
he thinks what might a miter matter?

Unfunny uncle, you who wore a
hat too big, or one too many,
tell us, can't you, are there any
stars inside your black fedora?

Aunt exemplary and slim,
with avernal eyes, we wonder
what slow changes they see under
their vast, shady, turned-down brim.

Max Ernst
THE HAT MAKES THE MAN

*1920. Cut-and-pasted paper, pencil, ink,
and watercolor on paper, 14 x 18".
The Museum of Modern Art, New York.
Purchase*

MY HAT

Stevie Smith

Mother said if I wore this hat
I should be certain to get off with the right sort of chap
Well look where I am now, on a desert island
With so far as I can see no one at all on hand
I know what has happened though I suppose Mother
    wouldn't see
This hat being so strong has completely run away with me
I had the feeling it was beginning to happen the moment I put
    it on
What a moment that was that I rose up, I rose up like a flying
    swan
As strong as a swan too, why see how far my hat has flown me
    away
It took us a night to come and then a night and a day
And all the time the swan wing in my hat waved beautifully
Ah, I thought, How this hat becomes me.
First the sea was dark but then it was pale blue
And still the wing beat and we flew and we flew
A night and a day and a night, and by the old right way
Between the sun and the moon we flew until morning day.
It is always early morning here on this peculiar island
The green grass grows into the sea on the dripping land
Am I glad I am here? Yes, well, I am,
It's nice to be rid of Father, Mother, and the young man
There's just one thing causes me a twinge of pain,
If I take my hat off, shall I find myself home again?
So in this early morning land I always wear my hat
Go home, you see, well I wouldn't run a risk like that.

Frances McLauglin-Gill
WOMAN REACHING FOR ANKLE WEARING PLAID
BERTOLI SUN HAT AND WIDE LEGLET ON CAPRI

1951. Courtesy Vogue

"My mother told me many stories"
   Arshile Gorky

My mother told me many stories
while I pressed my face into her long apron
with my eyes closed. . . .
Her stories and the embroidery on her apron
got confused in my mind with my eyes closed.
All my life her stories and her embroidery
keep unravelling pictures in my memory.
If I sit before a blank white canvas —

Arshile Gorky
HOW MY MOTHER'S EMBROIDERED APRON
UNFOLDS IN MY LIFE

*1944. Oil on canvas, 40 x 45". Seattle Art
Museum. Gift of Mr. And Mrs. Bagley Wright*

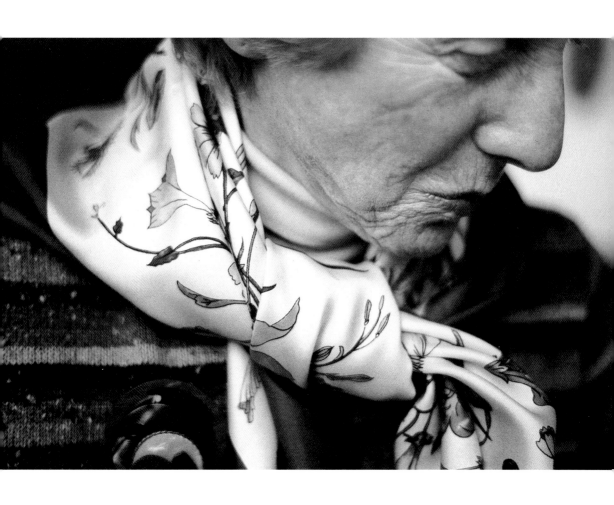

LONG TIME TOGETHER

Bob Arnold

4 dollars I paid
For this dark scarf
Of large red roses,

And love's fortune
Is that I had you
There with me, out

On the sidewalk to
Fold it, and wear
Around your neck

Jan Tymorek
MARJIE'S SCARF
1999

UPON JULIA'S CLOTHES

Robert Herrick

Whenas in silks my Julia goes,
Then, then, methinks, how sweetly flows
The liquefaction of her clothes!

Next, when I cast mine eyes and see
That brave vibration each way free,
– O how that glittering taketh me!

A. M. Cassandre
ADVERTISEMENT FOR LESUR

1946

A. M. Cassandre

A DANDY DUET

Both Anonymous

My boot-tops – those unerring marks of a *blade,*
With *champaigne* are polish'd, and *peach marmalade.*

My neckcloth, of course, forms my principal care,
For by that we criterions of elegance *swear,*
And costs me, each morning, some hours of flurry,
To make it *appear* to be tied in a *hurry.*

Robert Landry
FRED ASTAIRE DANCING

1945. Robert Landry/TimePix

Andy Warhol
LETTER TO THE WORLD (THE KICK),
MARTHA GRAHAM

*1986. Third of a portfolio of three screenprints on
lonox museum board, 36 x 36". The Andy Warhol
Foundation for the Visual Arts, Inc.*

THE PINK DRESS

Diane Wakoski

I could not wear that pink dress tonight.
The velvet one
lace tinting the cuffs with all
the coffee
of longing. My bare shoulder
slipping whiter
than foam
out of the night to remind me
of my own
vulnerability.

I could not wear that pink dress tonight
because it is a dress
that slips memories like
the hands
of obscene strangers
all over my body.
And in my fatigue I could not fight away the images
and their mean touching.

I couldn't wear that pink dress,
the velvet one you had made for me,
all year, you know.

I thought I would tonight because
once again
you have let me enter your house
and look at myself
some mornings
in your mirrors.
                    But
I could not wear that pink dress tonight
because it reminded me
of everything
that hurts.

It reminded me of a whole year
during which
I wandered,
a gypsy,
and could not come into your house.
It reminded me of the picture of a blond girl
you took with you to Vermont
and shared your woods with.
The pretty face you left over your bed to stare
at me
and remind me
each night
that you preferred her face to mine,
and which you left there to stare at me
even when you saw how it
broke me,
my calm,
like a stick smashing across my own
plain, lonesome face,
and a face which you only
took down
from your wall
after I had mutilated it
and pushed pins in it to get those
smug smiling eyes off my cold
winter
body.

I couldn't wear that pink dress tonight
because it reminded me
of the girl who made it,
whom you slept with
last year while I was sitting in hotel rooms
wondering why I had to live
with a face
so stony no man could love it.

I could not wear that pink dress
because it reminded me
of how I camp on your doorstep now,
still a gypsy,
still a colorful imaginative beggar
in my pink dress,
building a fire in the landowner's
woods, and my own fierceness
that deserts me
when a man
no, when you,
show a little care and concern
for my presence.

I could not wear that pink dress tonight.
It betrayed all that was strong in me.
The leather boots I wear to stomp through the world
and remind everyone
of the silver and gold and diamonds
from fairy tales
glittering in their lives.
And of the heavy responsibility
we all must bear
just being so joyfully alive
just letting the blood take its own course
in intact vessels
in veins.
That pink dress betrayed my one favorite image
      – the motorcyclist riding along the highway
        independent
        alone
        exhilarated with movement
        a blackbird
        more beautiful than any white ones.

But I went off
not wearing the pink dress,
thinking how much I love you
and how if a woman loves a man who does not
love her,
it is, as some good poet said,
a pain in the ass.
For both of them.

I went off thinking about all the girls
you preferred to me.
Leaving behind that dress,
remembering one of the colors
of pain
Remembering that my needs
affront you,
my face is not beautiful to you;
you would not share your woods with me.

And the irony
of my images.
That you are the motorcycle rider.
Not I.
I am perhaps,
at best,
the pink dress
thrown against the back
of the chair.
The dress I could not wear
tonight.

from A HUMUMENT:
A TREATED VICTORIAN NOVEL

Tom Phillips

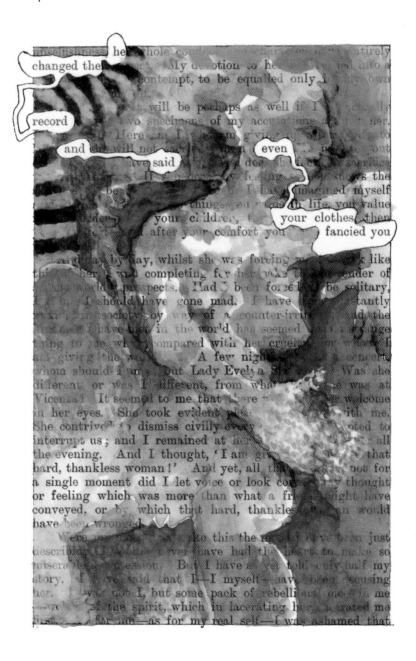

KERCHIEF

John Berger

In the morning
folded with its wild flowers
washed and ironed
it takes up little space in the drawer.

Shaking it open
she ties it round her head.

In the evening she pulls it off
and lets it fall
still knotted to the floor.

On a cotton scarf
among printed flowers
a working day
has written its dream.

Lucien Pissarro
RUTH GLEANS IN BOAZ'S FIELD
AFTER THE REAPERS

1896. Pen and ink, 4¼ x 3¹¹/₁₆".
V & A Picture Library, London

WHITE SUIT

Blaise Cendrars
translated by Ron Padgett

I stroll on deck in the white suit I bought in Dakar
On my feet the espadrilles bought in Villa García
I hold in my hand the Basque beret I brought from Biarritz
My pockets are filled with Caporal Ordinaires
From time to time I sniff my wooden cigarette case from Russia
I jingle the coins in my pocket and a pound sterling in gold
I have my big Calabrian handkerchief and some wax matches the big
    kind you find only in London
I'm clean washed scrubbed more than the deck
Happy as a king
Rich as a multimillionaire
Free as a man

Adelle Lutz
BIG SUIT
1984. Courtesy of Todo Mundo

NOVEMBER JEANS SONG

Hayden Carruth

Hey, hey, daddio,
Them old jeans is
    Going to go!

Rose Marie done put in a new
    Valve cover gasket,
Them jeans good for a whole nother
    10,000 mile.

Man the wood them jeans cut,
And split and trucked and stacked,
    No wonder the axe
Been yearning and drooping
Like the poor lone gander
    For them old jeans.

Look out, get set, let
    The woods take warning,
    Come six in the morning
    Me and them jeans is back,
What I mean *ready*,
We going to *go*
And don't care nothing for nothing
                    baby,
    Not even the snow.

A. Y. Owen
BOYS WITH THEIR FIRST CAR

1957. LIFE/TimePix

ODE TO MY SOCKS

Pablo Neruda
translated by Robert Bly

Maru Mori brought me
a pair
of socks
which she knitted herself
with her sheep-herder's hands,
two socks as soft
as rabbits.
I slipped my feet
into them
as though into
two
cases
knitted
with threads of
twilight
and goatskin.
Violent socks,
my feet were
two fish made of wool,
two long sharks
seablue, shot
through
by one golden thread,
two immense blackbirds,
two cannons,
my feet
were honored
in this way
by
these
heavenly
socks.
They were
so handsome
for the first time
my feet seemed to me
unacceptable
like two decrepit
firemen, firemen
unworthy
of that woven
fire,
of those glowing
socks.

Nevertheless
I resisted
the sharp temptation
to save them somewhere
as students
keep
fireflies,
as learned men
collect
sacred texts,
I resisted
the mad impulse
to put them
in a golden
cage
and each day give them
birdseed
and pieces of pink melon.
Like explorers
in the jungle who hand
over the very rare
green deer
to the spit
with remorse,
I stretched out
my feet
and pulled on
the magnificent
socks
and
then my shoes.

The moral
of my ode is this:
beauty is twice
beauty
and what is good is doubly
good
when it is a matter of two socks
made of wool
in winter.

CORRUGATED SOCKS

Vogue Knitting Socks,
Photograph by Brian Haus

ANGRY

ADMONITION   COURTSHIP   HESITATION

"On the Plains, the buffalo robe and later the trade blanket were important devices or props in the communication of subtle ideas or emotions."

— Patrick T. Houlahan in
Language of the Robe, by Robert Kapoun

Alice Fletcher and Francis La Flesche
THE OMAHA TRIBE

*1905–06. Bureau of American Ethnology,
Smithsonian Institution, Washington, D.C.*

FOUR-IN-HAND

John Hollander

Not Gordian nor a
Ghiordes warped
onto a bright
bit of yarn
from a rug
hiding in
high pile
No this is

not somehow

the knot of

the quotidian

which with an

as yet unmatched

panache he ties

mirrored mornings

to himself with A

holding together of

all of the reins of

the real for a time

A constant feeling of

widely bright stripes

to bind him through a

general zebra barriness

that comes between word

and word with interlinear

blanks Are these his hearts

blinds Or the binds

that almost

tie

Jim Dine A TIE IN A RED LANDSCAPE
1961. Oil and tie on canvas, 16 x 12". Richard Gray Gallery, Chicago

from ONE DESIGNING WOMEN

Pamela White Hadas

I. Imagine wearing something . . .
A well-dressed woman is closest to being naked. *

Imagine wearing something as if
you didn't. Imagine you could move as if
you did. Imagine dressing down to where
you start.
          It's not the body between the lines
in tact I hand you but the hands
that make and make the lines and let the body
move to move
          you – a woman dressed in myth –
made up and over and closest to being . . .

Done: *Integrity is mystery.*
          If you will,
imagine the perfect dress, invisible
with emphasis, a skin that, ripped, won't bleed.

Imagine! wearing something that dies on you –
if I wear a flower it's an artificial one.

*Attributed to Coco Chanel

CHANEL EVENING DRESS
c. 1935

THE PANTS OF THE
PASSER-BY

Lenard D. Moore

your pants gray, wrinkled
like chitterling –
yet wide as elephant ears,
flapping in evening wind;
still, you stroll down the sidewalk
as if you're in your Sunday best.

Bill Traylor
MAN BENDING BACK SMOKING

*1940/1942. Crayon and colored pencil on
cardboard, 15 x 12½". Private collection*

YELLOW VESTMENT

Patrick Kavanagh

Lately I have been travelling by a created guidance,
I invented a Superintendent, symbol henceforth vaster
Than Jupiter, Prometheus or a Chinese deity in alabaster.
For love's sake we must only consider whatever widens
The field of the faithful's activity. See over there
Water-lilies waiting to be enchanted by a folk song chanted.
On the road we walk nobody is unwanted;
With no hate in his heart or resentment each may wear
The arrogant air that goes with a yellow vestment.
Do not be worried about what the neighbours will say,
Deliver your judgment, you are independent
Of the man in the pub whose word is essential to happiness,
Who gives your existence. O sing to me some roundelay
And wear with grace the power-invoking habit.

Henri Matisse
DESIGN FOR LITURGICAL VESTMENTS
FOR THE VENCE CHAPEL

1950–51. Gouache on paper cutout.
Musée Matisse, Nice

MY SHOES

Charles Simic

Shoes, secret face of my inner life:
Two gaping toothless mouths,
Two partly decomposed animal skins
Smelling of mice-nests.

My brother and sister who died at birth
Continuing their existence in you,
Guiding my life
Toward their incomprehensible innocence.

What use are books to me
When in you it is possible to read
The Gospel of my life on earth
And still beyond, of things to come?

I want to proclaim the religion
I have devised for your perfect humility
And the strange church I am building
With you as the altar.

Ascetic and maternal, you endure:
Kin to oxen, to Saints, to condemned men,
With your mute patience, forming
The only true likeness of myself.

Robert Rauschenberg
ROME FLEA MARKET

1952

THE SHIRT

Jane Kenyon

The shirt touches his neck
and smooths over his back.
It slides down his sides.
It even goes down below his belt —
down into his pants.
Lucky shirt.

Raoul Dufy
FISHERMAN WITH A NET

1914. Oil on canvas, 86¼ x 26". Musée
National d'Art Moderne, Centre National d'Art
et de Culture Georges Pompidou, Paris

OVERALLS
from *Let Us Now Praise Famous Men*

James Agee

Overalls.

They are pronounced overhauls.

Try – I cannot write of it here – to imagine and to know, as against other gar-
ments, the difference of their feeling against your body; drawn-on, and bibbed
on the whole belly and chest, naked from the kidneys up behind, save for
broad crossed straps, and slung by these straps from the shoulders; the slanted
pockets on each thigh, the deep square pockets on each buttock; the complex
and slanted structures, on the chest, of the pockets shaped for pencils, rulers,
and watches; the coldness of sweat when they are young, and their stiffness;
their sweetness to the skin and pleasure of sweating when they are old; the thin
metal buttons of the fly; the lifting aside of the straps and the deep slipping
downward in defecation; the belt some men use with them to steady their
middles; the swift, simple, and inevitably supine gestures of dressing and of
undressing, which, as is less true of any other garment, are those of harnessing
and of unharnessing the shoulders of a tired and hard-used animal.

They are round as stovepipes in the legs (though some wives, told to, crease
them).

In the strapping across the kidneys they again resemble work harness, and
in their crossed straps and tin buttons.

And in the functional pocketing of their bib, a harness modified to the
convenience of a used animal of such high intelligence that he has use for tools.

And in their whole stature: full covering of the cloven strength of the legs
and thighs and of the loins; then nakedness and harnessing behind, naked
along the flanks; and in front the short, squarely tapered, powerful towers of
the belly and chest to above the nipples.

And on this façade, the cloven halls for the legs, the strong-seamed, struc-
tured opening for the genitals, the broad horizontal at the waist, the slant thigh
pockets, the buttons at the point of each hip and on the breast, the geometric
structures of the usages of the simpler trades – the complexed seams of utilitar-
ian pockets which are so brightly picked out against darkness when the seam-
threadings, double and triple stitched, are still white, so that a new suit of
overalls has among its beauties those of a blueprint: and they are the map of a
working man.

Walker Evans MAN IN OVERALLS from *Let Us Now Praise Famous Men*
1936. Reproduced from the Collections of the Library of Congress, Washington, D.C.

SHE HAS A BODY ON HER DRESS

Blaise Cendrars
translated by Ron Padgett

A woman's body is as bumpy as my skull
Glorious
If you're embodied with a little spirit
Fashion designers have a stupid job
As stupid as phrenology
My eyes are kilos that weigh the sensuality of women

Everything that recedes, stands out comes forward into the death
The stars deepen the sky
The colors undress
"She has a body on her dress"
Beneath her arms heathers hands lunules and pistils when the waters
    flow into her back with its blue-green shoulder blades
Her belly a moving disk
The double-bottomed hull of her breasts goes under the bridge of
    rainbows
Belly
Disk
Sun
The perpendicular cries of the colors fall on her thighs
The Sword of Saint Michael

There are hands that reach out
In its train the animal all the eyes all the fanfares all the regulars at the
    Bal Bullier
And on her hip
The poet's signature

Sonia Delaunay
ROBE POÈME (CETTE FEMME ETERNELLE)

*1922. Watercolor, 14 x 11½". Bibliothèque
Nationale de France*

JUST HOW DO YOU SUPPOSE THAT ALICE KNOWS

Calvin Trillin

Just how do you suppose that Alice knows
So much about what's au courant in clothes?
You wouldn't really think that she's the sort
To know much more than whether skirts are short
Or long again, or somewhere in between.
She's surely not the sort who would be seen
In front-row seats at Paris fashion shows.
In fact, she looks at that sort down her nose.
For her to read a fashion mag would seem
As out of synch as reading *Field & Stream.*
Biographies are what she reads instead.
And yet she has, in detail, in her head
Whose indigos are drawing "ooh"s and "oh"s.
Just how do you suppose that Alice knows?

We're leaving, and I'll ask her, once we've gone,
"What *was* that thing that whatzername had on?
It lacked a back. The front was sort of lined
With gauzy stuff. It seemed to be the kind
Of frock that might be worn by Uncle Meyer
If he played Blanche in 'Streetcar Named Desire.'"
And Alice knows. She knows just who designed
The rag and why some folks are of a mind
To buy this *schmattameister's* frilly things
For what a small Brancusi usually brings.
She mentions something newly chic this year.
To me it looked like antique fishing gear.
I'm stunned, as if she'd talked in Urdu prose.
Just how do you suppose that Alice knows?

She gets no E-mail info on design.
(She's au courant but, so far, not on-line.)
No fashion maven tells her what is kitsch.
She goes to no symposium at which
She learns why some designer's models pose
As Navajos or folks from U.F.O.s.
I know that women have no special gene
Providing knowledge of the fashion scene,
The way that men all have, without a doubt,
The chromosome for garbage-taking-out.
And yet she's fashion-conscious to her toes.
Does she divine these things? Does she osmose
What's in the air concerning hose and bows?
Just how do you suppose that Alice knows?

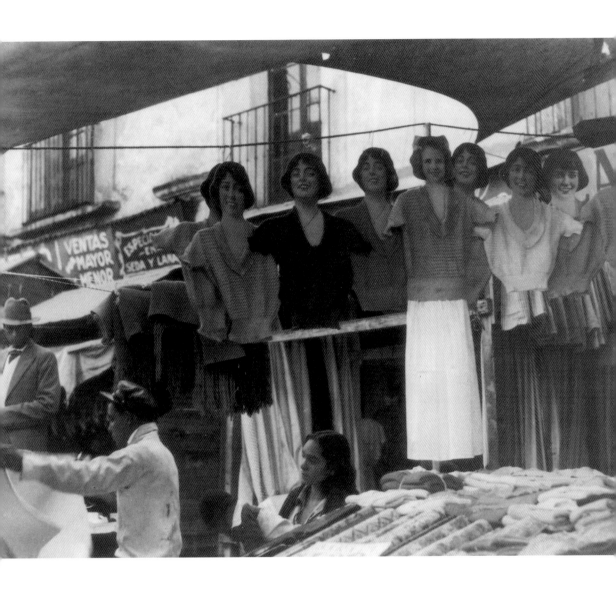

Manuel Alvarez-Bravo
LAUGHING MANNEQUINS

*c. 1932. Silver gelatin print. The Art Institute of Chicago.
Julien Levy Collection, gift of Jean Levy and the estate of
Julien Levy*

from HER SIGNATURE HERSELF

Theodore Enslin

My girl's a weave of many things   I
do not know the names of all the threads
or lap or warp which make for colors
several in delight   yet supple.
It is cloth that will not fade
the dye was fated not to bleach
or soak away.   Her heat has burned it in
and if I look to see more there than
what she shows me   I will find
a pleasure in each shadow
taking form for what is not
informed suggestion   is so woven.

Romare Bearden
LA PRIMAVERA

1967. Collage on board, 44 x 56".
Private collection

IN MY GLOVE OF GOLD

Edgard Braga
translated by Edwin Morgan

in my glove of gold   in my glove of silver
i hid men and nations   i hid my shame

        in my glove of stone
        i hid my death

        in my glove of iron
        i hid my silence

knight-at-arms knight-at-arms   knight-at-arms knight-at-arms
throw your glove to the winds   throw your glove to the winds

        knight-at-arms knight-at-arms
        throw your glove to the winds

        knight-at-arms knight-at-arms
        keep your glove
                keep
               the winds

Gustav Klimt
LIFE IS A STRUGGLE (THE GOLDEN KNIGHT)

1903. Oil, tempera, and gold on canvas, 39⅜ x 39⅜".
Aichi Prefectural Museum of Art, Nagoya, Japan

ON A PAIR OF GARTERS

Sir John Davies

Go, loving woodbine, clip with lovely grace
Those two sweet plants which bear the flowers of love;
Go, silken vines, those tender elms embrace
Which flourish still although their roots do move.
As soon as you possess your blessed places
You are advancèd and ennobled more
Than diadems, which were white silken laces
That ancient kings about their forehead wore.
Sweet bands, take heed lest you ungently bind,
Or with your strictness make too deep a print:
Was never tree had such a tender rind,
Although her inward heart be hard as flint.
And let your knots be fast and loose at will:
She must be free, though I stand bounden still.

Edward Steichen
MODEL WEARING ELASTIC
AND SATIN CORSET WITH A
LACE BRASSIERE

1930. Courtesy Vogue

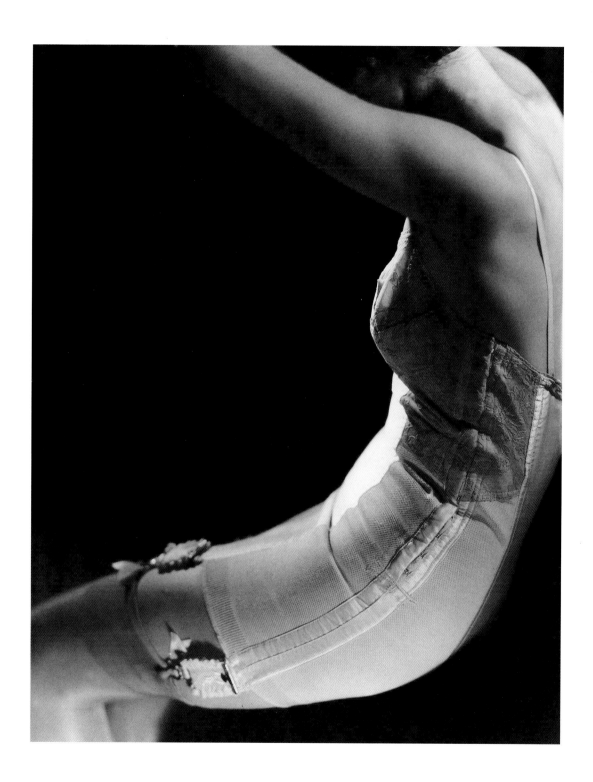

from *TALE OF GENJI*

Murasaki Shikibu
translated by Liza Crihfield Dalby

When the colors of a robe do not
match the seasons, the flowers of
Spring and the Autumn tints, then
the whole effort is futile as the dew.

Jodi Cobb
GEISHAS

1995

PONCHO: RITUAL DRESS

Cecilia Vicuña

hilo de agua
thread of water

hilo de vida
thread of life

they say woolly animals
are born high in the
mountain springs

water and fiber
are one

wool & cotton
downy fiber
an open hand

the Cotton Mother textile goddess in Chavín is a plant creature with snake
feet, eyes and heart radiating from the center like a sun

the poncho
is a book
a woven
message

a metaphor
spun

white stones found in the mist, the *illa* and the *enqaychu* are the emblems
of the vital force within the woolly animals themselves but only the poor
and haggard can find them by the springs.

Patt Hill
ECUADOR

*1989. The Textile Museum,
Washington, D.C.*

SPORTING BEASLEY

Sterling A. Brown

Good glory, give a look at Sporting Beasley
Strutting, oh my Lord.

> Tophat cocked one side his bulldog head,
> Striped four-in-hand, and in his buttonhole
> A red carnation; Prince Albert coat
> Form-fitting, corset like; vest snugly filled,
> Gray morning trousers, spotless and full-flowing,
> White spats and a cane.

Step it, Mr. Beasley, oh step it till the sun goes down.

    Forget the snippy clerks you wait upon,
    Tread clouds of glory above the heads of pointing children,
    Oh, Mr. Peacock, before the drab barnfowl of the world.

    Forget the laughter when at the concert
    You paced down the aisle, your majesty,
    Down to Row A, where you pulled out your opera glasses.

    Majesty. . . .

    It's your turn now, Sporting Beasley,
    Step it off.

    The world is a ragbag; the world
    Is full of heathens who haven't seen the light;
    Do it, Mr. Missionary.

Great glory, give a look.

    Oh Jesus, when this brother's bill falls due,
    When he steps off the chariot
    And flicks the dust from his patent leathers with his silk handkerchief,
    When he stands in front of the jasper gates, patting his tie,

    And then paces in
    Cane and knees working like well-oiled slow-timed pistons;

Lord help us, give a *look* at him.
Don't make him dress up in no night gown, Lord.
Don't put no fuss and feathers on his shoulders, Lord.

Let him know it's heaven.

Let him keep his hat, his vest, his elkstooth, and everything.

Let him have his spats and cane
Let him have his spats and cane.

INVISIBLE MENDING

C. K. Williams

Three women old as angels,
bent as ancient apple trees,
who, in a storefront window,
with magnifying glasses,
needles fine as hair, and shining
scissors, parted woof from warp
and pruned what would in
human tissue have been sick.

Abrasions, rents and frays,
slits and chars and acid
splashes, filaments that gave
way of their own accord
from the stress of spanning
tiny, trifling gaps, but which
in a wounded psyche
make a murderous maze.

Their hands as hard as horn,
their eyes as keen as steel,
the threads they worked with
must have seemed as thick
as ropes on ships, as cables
on a crane, but still their heads
would lower, their teeth bare
to nip away the raveled ends.

Only sometimes would they
lift their eyes to yours to show
how much lovelier than these twists
of silk and serge the garments
of the mind are, yet how much
more benign their implements
than mind's procedures
of forgiveness and repair.

And in your loneliness you'd notice
how really very gently they'd take
the fabric to its last, with what
solicitude gather up worn edges
to be bound, with what severe
but kind detachment wield
their amputating shears:
forgiveness, and repair.

Jan Tymorek
STELLA'S HANDS

1989

74

COURTESY CALL

John Updike

We again thank you for your esteemed order and now wish to advise you
that the clothes are awaiting the pleasure of your visit.

– card from a London tailor

My clothes leaped up when I came in
    My trousers cried, "Oh, is it
Our own, our prince?" and split their pleats
    At the pleasure of my visit.

My jacket tried to dance with joy
    But lacked the legs; it screamed,
"Though our confusion is deplored,
    Your order is esteemed!"

"Dear clothes," I cooed, "at ease. Down, please.
    Adjust your warp and weft."
Said they, "We love you." I: "I know,
    I was advised," and left.

Jim Dine
WHITE SUIT #2 (SELF PORTRAIT)

*1964. Oil and charcoal on canvas with metal
chain and padlock, electrical cords and outlets,
light bulb, magnifying glass, wire and metal
hooks. 71½ x 72". Courtesy of Pace Wildenstein*

HENRY DE MONTHERLANT

Guy Davenport

Such heavy leather shoes for legs
so young and slender to end in,
the only bulk to a body
so lightly clad. To pull them from
his messy gym bag where they've lain
under muddy and grass-stained shorts,
is to hear the coach's whistle
slice the air, the field crack, to take
from the private musk of a sack
the cold light of a winter day
and hold victory in my hands.
So inert, so slight to the eye,
these flying kicking, living shoes
obeyed the fierce will of a boy
who could fight back a hero's tears.
Still oiled, still spattered with dried mud,
they've kept their strong seaweed odor.
In their scuffed heft, copper grommets,
and essence of brute elegance,
they are as noble as the field
they trod and the boy who wore them.
The ankles are bulged like the boss
of a Greek shield, the instep his.
Could I not know whose shoes these were?
To cup the hard heels in my hands
is to feel them full of bright fire.

Annie Leibovitz
JULIE FOUDY, SEMINOLE COUNTY SPORTS
TRAINING CENTER, SANFORD, FLORIDA

1996. Courtesy of Leibovitz Studio, Inc.

"The suit I wore tomorrow"

César Vallejo
translated by Edward Dorn and Gordon Brotherston

The suit I wore tomorrow
my washerwoman has not washed:
once she washed it in her otiline* veins,
in the fountain of her heart, and today
I'd better not wonder   was I leaving
my suit muddy with injustice.

Now that there's no one going to the water,
the canvas for pluming stiffens in
my sampler, and all the things
on the night-table from so much what'll become of me,
are all not mine there
at my side.

               They remained her property,
smoothed down, brothersealed with her wheat goodness.

And if only I knew whether she'll come back;
and if only I knew what morrow she'll come in
and hand me my washed clothes, that soul
washerwoman of mine. What morrow she'll come in
satisfied, blooming with handiwork, happy
at proving she *does* know, that she is able
               LIKE HOW COULDN'T SHE BE
to blue and iron out all chaos.

**From the proper name Otilia; Vallejo parted from a
woman of this name in 1919.*

Diego Rivera
WASHERWOMAN WITH ZOPILOTES

*1928. Oil and encaustic on canvas, 22 x 16⅞".
Mary-Ann Martin/Fine Art, New York*

BLACK JACKETS

Thom Gunn

In the silence that prolongs the span
Rawly of music when the record ends,
 The red-haired boy who drove a van
In weekday overalls but, like his friends,

 Wore cycle boots and jacket here
To suit the Sunday hangout he was in,
 Heard, as he stretched back from his beer,
Leather creak softly round his neck and chin.

 Before him, on a coal-black sleeve
Remote exertion had lined, scratched, and burned
 Insignia that could not revive
The heroic fall or climb where they were earned.

 On the other drinkers bent together,
Concocting selves for their impervious kit,
 He saw it as no more than leather
Which, taut across the shoulders grown to it,

Sent through the dimness of a bar
As sudden and anonymous hints of light
 As those that shipping give, that are
Now flickers in the Bay, now lost in night.

 He stretched out like a cat, and rolled
The bitterish taste of beer upon his tongue,
 And listened to a joke being told:
The present was the things he stayed among.

 If it was only loss he wore,
He wore it to assert, with fierce devotion,
 Complicity and nothing more.
He recollected his initiation,

And one especially of the rites.
For on his shoulders they had put tattoos:
 The group's name on the left, The Knights,
And on the right the slogan Born To Lose.

Andy Warhol
MARLON

*1966. Silkscreen ink on canvas, 81 x 50". The
Andy Warhol Museum. Purchase, with funds
from the Andy Warhol Foundation for the Visual
Arts, Inc., and Dia Center for the Arts, 1999*

82

Queen of the Carnival

from LA DERNIÈRE MODE

Stéphane Mallarmé
translated by Jan Tymorek

I define the tradition that all ball gowns fulfill as:
rendering nimble, vaporous and ethereal, by that superior way of walking called dance,
the goddess wrapped in their clouds.

Clarence John Laughlin
THE APPARITION NO. 9

1946. The Historic New Orleans Collection

DELIGHT IN DISORDER

Robert Herrick

A sweet disorder in the dresse
Kindles in cloathes a wantonnesse:
A Lawne about the shoulders thrown
Into a fine distraction:
An erring Lace, which here and there
Enthralls the Crimson Stomacher:
A Cuffe neglectfull, and thereby
Ribbands to flow confusedly:
A winning wave (deserving Note)
In the tempestuous petticote:
A carelesse shooe-string, in whose tye
I see a wilde civility:
Doe more bewitch me, then when Art
Is too precise in every part.

from CENT SONNETS

Boris Vian
translated by Jan Tymorek

Now a zazou* was strolling on rue Gay-Lussac
With cheeks all aglow, blithe mustache of down.
A true zazou was he, wearing hat chocolate brown,
Suede shoes, long jacket and pants like a sack.

*In Paris during the years 1939 to 1943, "Zazous embodied the swing culture
down to their fingernails." – *A History of Men's Fashion,* by Farid Chenoune

YOUNG "ZAZOU" DANCING

c. 1939

DANDELION WOMAN

Jonathan Greene

Head and neck
rising out of a tree of a dress

sculptural, planted in a field
of matching flowers

the photographer's
instructions to tilt the head just so

this dandelion woman
looking to some distance within.

Robin Barcus
DANDELION DRESS

*1999. Wire mesh dress form
and dandelions, 10'*

THE SATIN DRESS

Dorothy Parker

Needle, needle, dip and dart,
Thrusting up and down,
Where's the man could ease a heart
Like a satin gown?

See the stitches curve and crawl
Round the cunning seams –
Patterns thin and sweet and small
As a lady's dreams.

Wantons go in bright brocades;
Brides in organdie;
Gingham's for the plighted maid;
Satin's for the free!

Wool's to line a miser's chest;
Crape's to calm the old;
Velvet hides an empty breast;
Satin's for the bold!

Lawn is for a bishop's yoke;
Linen's for a nun;
Satin is for wiser folk –
Would the dress were done!

Satin glows in candlelight –
Satin's for the proud!
They will say who watch at night,
"What a fine shroud!"

Erwin Blumenfeld
SATIN DRESS

1938. Courtesy Vogue France

from PIECES OF SUMMER

August Kleinzahler

On the subway escalator,
eyes averted,
pants snug as the skin of half-ripe pears

In pastel rooms all through this melting world
love-thoughts, like cuttings,
have begun to take

Joseph Cornell
ALLEGORY OF INNOCENCE

*1956. Cut-and-pasted papers on paper
mounted on composition board, covered
with antique glass, 15¼ x 12¼". The
Museum of Modern Art, New York.
Purchase*

THE PLAID DRESS

Edna St. Vincent Millay

Strong sun, that bleach
The curtains of my room, can you not render
Colourless this dress I wear? –
This violent plaid
Of purple angers and red shames; the yellow stripe
Of thin but valid treacheries; the flashy green of kind
     deeds done
Through indolence, high judgments given here in haste;
The recurring checker of the serious breach of taste?

No more uncoloured than unmade,
I fear, can be this garment that I may not doff;
Confession does not strip it off,
To send me homeward eased and bare;

All through the formal, unoffending evening, under
     the clean
Bright hair,
Lining the subtle gown . . . it is not seen,
But it is there.

Egon Schiele
GERTI SCHIELE IN A PLAID GARMENT

*c. 1908–09. Charcoal and tempera,
52¾ x 20¾". The Minneapolis Institute of
Arts. The John R. Van Derlip Fund and
gift of Dr. Otto Kallir*

BEDTIME

Ian Hamilton Finlay

So put your nightdress on
It is so white and long
And your sweet night-face
Put it on also please
It is the candle-flame
It is the flame above
Whose sweet shy shame
My love, I love, I love.

Alfred Steiglitz
GEORGIA O'KEEFFE (IN WHITE ROBE,
RECLINING WITH HANDS ON FOREHEAD)

c. 1918. Palladium print, 7 1/8 x 9". The
Metropolitan Museum of Art. Gift of Georgia
O'Keeffe through the generosity of The
Georgia O'Keeffe Foundation and Jennifer
and Joseph Duke, 1997

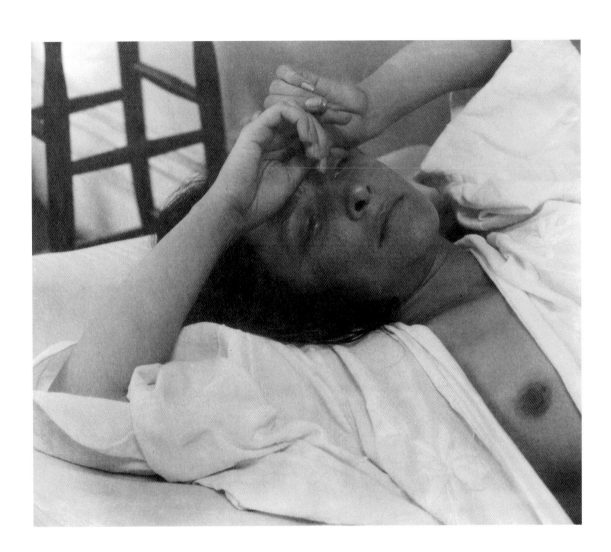

SLIPPERS ON HER FEET

Shen Yüeh
translated by Anne Birrell

Up cinnabar court fluttering,
Down jade halls swiftly tapping,
They pirouette and her pearl belt tinkles,
Early scent creeps from her broidered coat.
Skirts open near the dance floor,
Sleeves brush round the song hall.
They sigh for their indifferent mistress:
'We're tossed aside when she enters silk curtains'.

Anonymous
IMPERIAL WINTER DRAGON ROBE

*Early 19th century. Embroidered silk.
University of Michigan Museum of Art,
Gift of Elizabeth Henshaw Gasper Brown
in memory of Horace William and Helen
Louise Henshaw*

MY OLD GRAY SWEATER

James Laughlin

in the back of the closet what
will you do with it the one with

buttons down the front the heavy
one I used to wear when I could

still cut firewood what will you
do with it the Salvation Army I

guess some worthy & needy man
can still get a lot of use out

of it but you know I'd really
rather not please take it out

into the woods and nail it to
that big oak Gary jokes that

he wants to re-enter the food
chain he wants to be eaten by

a bear I'd like my sweater just
to rot away in the woodlands let

the birds peck at it and build
their nests with the gray wool

please nail me to the big oak.

Jan Tymorek
CHRIS'S WOODPILE
1999

from *I SING THE BODY ELECTRIC*

Walt Whitman

But the expression of a well-made man appears not only in
      his face,
It is in his limbs and joints also, it is curiously in the joints
      of his hips and wrists,
It is in his walk, the carriage of his neck, the flex of his
      waist and knees, dress does not hide him,
The strong sweet quality he has strikes through the cotton
      and broadcloth,
To see him pass conveys as much as the best poem,
      perhaps more. . . .

Barbara Morgan
SPRING ON MADISON SQUARE

*1938. Courtesy of Barbara Morgan
Archives*

104

INDEX OF POETS

Agee, James, 56
Arnold, Bob, 25

Berger, John, 35
Bishop, Elizabeth, 19
Braga, Edgard, 64
Brown, Sterling A., 72–73

Carruth, Hayden, 38
Cendrars, Blaise, 36, 59
Creeley, Robert, 10

Davenport, Guy, 78
Davies, Sir John, 66

Enslin, Theodore, 62

Finlay, Ian Hamilton, 98

Greene, Jonathan, 91
Gunn, Thom, 82

Hadas, Pamela White, 46
Herrick, Robert, 26, 86
Hollander, John, 44

Kavanagh, Patrick, 50
Kenyon, Jane, 55
Kleinzahler, August, 95

Laughlin, James, 103

Mallarmé, Stéphane, 85
Millay, Edna St. Vincent, 96
Moore, Lenard D., 49

Neruda, Pablo, 40
Nichols, Grace, 16
Niedecker, Lorine, 14

Parker, Dorothy, 92
Peacock, Molly, 6
Phillips, Tom, 33

Simic, Charles, 52
Shikibu, Murasaki, 68
Smith, Stevie, 20

Trillin, Calvin, 60

Updike, John, 76

Vallejo, César, 81
Vian, Boris, 88
Vicuña, Cecilia, 70

Wakoski, Diane, 31–32
Whitman, Walt, 104
Wieder, Laurance, 8
Williams, C. K., 74

Yüeh, Shen, 100

Zisquit, Linda, 13

INDEX OF ARTISTS

Alvarez-Bravo, Manuel, 61

Barcus, Robin, 90–91
Bearden, Romare, 62–63
Beaton, Cecil, 9
Blumenfeld, Erwin, 93

Cassandre, A. M., 27
Cobb, Jodi, 68–69
Colin, Paul, 72
Cornell, Joseph, 94
Czettel, Ladislas, 2

Delaunay, Sonia, 58
Dine, Jim, 45, 77
Dufy, Raoul, 54

Ernst, Max, 18
Evans, Walker, 57

Fletcher, Alice, 42–43

Gilardi, Pier Celestino, 7
Gorky, Arshile, 23

Hill, Patt, 71

Katav-Arieli, Dalia, 12
Klimt, Gustav, 11, 65

La Flesche, Francis, 42–43
Landry, Robert, 29
Laughlin, Clarence John, 84
Leibovitz, Annie, 78–79
Lutz, Adelle, 37

Matisse, Henri, 51
McLaughlin-Gill, Frances, 21
Morgan, Barbara, 104–05

Owen, A. Y., 39

Phillips, Tom, 33
Pissarro, Lucien, 34

Rauschenberg, Robert, 53
Rivera, Diego, 80

Sargent, John Singer, 87
Schiele, Egon, 15, 97
Steichen, Edward, 67
Steiglitz, Alfred, 99

Traylor, Bill, 48
Tymorek, Jan, 17, 24, 75, 102

Warhol, Andy, 30, 83

For my mother, Stella Tymorek

EDITOR: Elisa Urbanelli
DESIGNER: Ellen Nygaard Ford

Library of Congress Cataloging-in-Publication Data

Clotheslines : a collection of poetry and art / edited by Stan
Tymorek.
        p. cm.
    ISBN 0–8109–5732–9
      1. Clothing and dress – Poetry. 2. Poetry – 20th century –
Translations into English. I. Tymorek, Stan.

PN6110.C59 C58 2000
808.81'9355—dc21   00–061842

Published in 2001 by Harry N. Abrams, Incorporated, New York

Printed and bound in Hong Kong

Harry N. Abrams, Inc.
100 Fifth Avenue
New York, N.Y. 10011
www.abramsbooks.com

JACKET FRONT:
Copyright © 2001 L & M Services B.V. Amsterdam 971103

PAGE 2:
Ladislas Czettel
GRAY DRESS WITH TYPEWRITER KEYS FOR
SKIRT AND LARGE BLACK BOW HEADDRESS

c. 1928. Gouache, 8 x 10". Hargrett Rare Book
and Manuscript Library, University of Georgia Libraries